KALEIDOSCOPE

How States Make Laws

Suzanne LeVert

BENCHMARK BOOKS

MARSHALL CAVENDISH
NEW YORK

Benchmark Books
Marshall Cavendish
99 White Plains Rd.
Tarrytown, NY 10591
www.marshallcavendish.com

Library of Congress Cataloging-in-Publication Data

LeVert, Suzanne.
  How states make laws / by Suzanne LeVert.
    p. cm. — (Kaleidoscope)
Summary: An examination of the legislative branch on the state level, including the legislative houses and the
process through which a bill becomes a law. Includes bibliographical references and index.
  ISBN 0-7614-1595-5
  1. Legislative bodies—United States—States—Juvenile literature. 2. Legislation—United States—States—Juvenile
literature. 3. State governments—United States—Juvenile literature. [1. Legislative bodies—United States—States.
2. Legislation. 3. Law. 4. State governments.] I. Title. II. Series: Kaleidoscope (Tarrytown, N.Y.)

JK2488.L48 2004
328.73'077—dc21
                                            2003001895

Photo research by Anne Burns Images

Cover photo: AP Photo/John Mummert

The photographs in this book are used with permission and through the courtesy of:
Corbis: title page; Reuters New Media Inc., 7, 27, 28; Paul A. Souders, 15; Alan Schein Photography, 16; Bob Rowan,
19; Becky Luigart-Stayner, 20; AFP, 23, 39; Bettman, 31; Ted Spiegel, 35. *Getty Images*: Chris Hondros/Newsmakers,
8; Joe Raedle, 32. *State Archives of Oregon*: 11, 43. *AP Photos*: Toby Talbot, 12; Mark Humphrey, 24; Kathy Willens,
40; John Mummert, 36.

Series design by Adam Mietlowski

Printed in Italy

6 5 4 3 2 1

Contents

Executive Branch

Enforce Laws

— Governor

— Executive Officers

Legislative Branch

Create & Enact Laws

— Senators

— Representatives

Judicial Branch

Interpret & Apply Laws

— Supreme Court Justices

— Lower Court Judges

How States Make Laws

Like America's federal—or national—government, its state governments are divided into three branches. The **executive branch**, led by the governor, enforces the laws, or makes sure they are obeyed. The **judicial branch** interprets the laws. It is the **legislative branch** that writes and **enacts** the laws that must be followed by every citizen in the state.

◄ *Like the federal—or national—government, state governments are also divided into three branches. It is the legislative branch that creates each state's laws.*

The men and women who work as state legislators represent the people who elect them. They work together to create programs and laws that help improve the lives of the state's residents. To do this, legislators talk and listen to the residents. Often citizens have ideas for new laws or ways their state can be better run.

State lawmakers must work for the good of all the state's citizens. Here, a representative holds a copy of the oath some legislators take promising to protect and defend the state constitution. ▶

Who Serves

Every state has a written **constitution**. It is a document that sets up how the government is run. It outlines what is required of someone who wants to become a state senator or representative.

There are only a certain number of senators and representatives who can serve in each state's legislature. The number elected in each house, or branch of the legislature, is usually based on a **census**. A census is an official count of the U.S. population. It totals the number of people who live in each city and town. The result of the census tells the legislature how many representatives and senators can serve each district in the state.

◄ *The government takes a census usually every ten years. Here, census takers in New York City meet before going door to door to count the number of people living there.*

The Legislature

Every state except Nebraska has a legislature with two houses. This two-house system is known as a **bicameral legislature**. States have chosen different names for their law-making bodies. Most call it the state legislature, but seventeen states call it the general assembly and two call it the general court. In states with two houses, the upper chamber, or part, is known as the **senate**. Most states call the lower chamber the **house of representatives**. Four states call it the assembly, and three call it the house of delegates.

Every state has its own capitol, the building where the state legislature usually meets. Oregon's state capitol, located in Salem, was first used in 1938.

In most states, senators serve for four years. Only in a few states do they serve for two. The senate elects a president who is in charge of the sessions. Another senate official is the **president pro tempore**. This officer assists the president of the senate and takes his or her place if the president cannot attend. Members of most state houses of representatives serve for two years. In many states, senators and representatives work together to make new laws. But in others, each house of the legislature works separately.

◀ *The state legislature helps to create state laws. Most states have two branches of the legislature. They are usually called the senate and the house of representatives.*

The job of the state legislature is to make and pass laws. These laws affect almost every part of our lives. For example, state legislatures decide if we must wear seat belts while riding in cars. They also tell us the age at which we can first learn how to drive. Other laws are added as the state faces new challenges. For instance, many state legislatures made laws to increase the budgets of police and fire departments after the terrorist attacks of September 11, 2001.

One of the many jobs of state legislatures is to make laws the state's drivers must follow. ▶

How a Bill Is Passed

Every year state legislatures consider more than 100,000 bills, or ideas for laws. Of this number, the legislatures will turn about 25,000, or 25 percent, of these bills into laws. That is about 130 times the number of laws the U.S. Congress in Washington, D.C., creates every year.

◀ *The U.S. Capitol in Washington, D.C., houses the national legislature, made up of senators and representatives from every state in the nation.*

State legislatures must follow a certain **procedure**, or set of steps, in order to pass laws. An example may help you better understand the process. In Minnesota a group of schoolchildren decided that the state needed to have an official state muffin. Only a few states have an official muffin. Massachusetts selected the corn muffin, and New York chose the apple muffin. The Minnesota schoolchildren decided that the blueberry muffin would be the best choice for their state. Lots of wild blueberries grow in the northern part of Minnesota.

Every citizen—young and old—can have a voice in the way their states work. Here, a group of students gets a lesson in government on the grounds of their state capitol.

The first step the children took was to share their idea with a member of the state's house of representatives. He became the sponsor of a bill to make the blueberry muffin Minnesota's official muffin. A sponsor writes the bill and presents it to the legislature. In Minnesota the two houses of the legislature work separately. So the sponsor of this bill presented it to the house of representatives first. Members of the house formed a committee to consider whether or not to adopt a state muffin. When it came time to decide on the bill, the house voted in favor of it.

Schoolchildren from Minnesota worked with their state legislature to make the blueberry muffin the official state muffin.

But before a bill can become a law, both houses of the legislature must vote in favor of it. Once the bill passes the house of representatives, it goes before the full senate for a vote. Sometimes the senate disagrees with all or part of a bill. When that happens, members might form another kind of committee, sometimes called a caucus, to discuss the bill further. In the case of the Minnesota muffin, the senate voted in favor of the bill after reading the school-children's letters.

Often committees are formed to look into a bill in more detail. The members of the committee can discuss the bill and focus on parts of it they want changed.

If both the senate and the house of representatives vote in favor of a bill, the bill then goes to the **governor**. The governor either signs the bill or **vetoes**, or rejects, the bill. If the governor vetoes the bill, the state legislature can still make it a law if enough members of the legislature vote in favor of it. In most states, two-thirds of each house must vote for the bill for it to become a law.

The legislature often reverses a governor's decision to veto, or reject, a bill. Here, Tennessee's house of representatives works to overturn the governor's veto of the state's budget.

In the case of Minnesota's muffin bill, the governor was in full support. He signed the bill into law. The blueberry muffin became the state's official muffin. Although each state has its own rules and steps, every bill made into law goes through a process much like this one.

Once a bill is signed, it becomes a part of state law.

The Governor and the Legislature

The governor is the head of the executive branch of the state government. He or she does more than reject or approve laws. He or she can propose laws to the legislature. The governor also has the power to have the legislature meet whenever there is an emergency.

Florida state senator Lisa Carlton waits as state representative Johnnie Byrd signs a document from the governor. Both lawmakers needed to approve an emergency session of the state legislature.

One of the governor's most important jobs is to share his or her ideas of how the state should be run. He or she also makes reports to the legislature, often concerning how much money the state has and how it should be spent. The governor and the legislature work together to make the state a better place in which to live.

Douglas Wilder, then governor of Virginia, speaks to the state legislature during his State of the Commonwealth address. Governors often work closely with state legislatures to gain support for laws, policies, and programs.

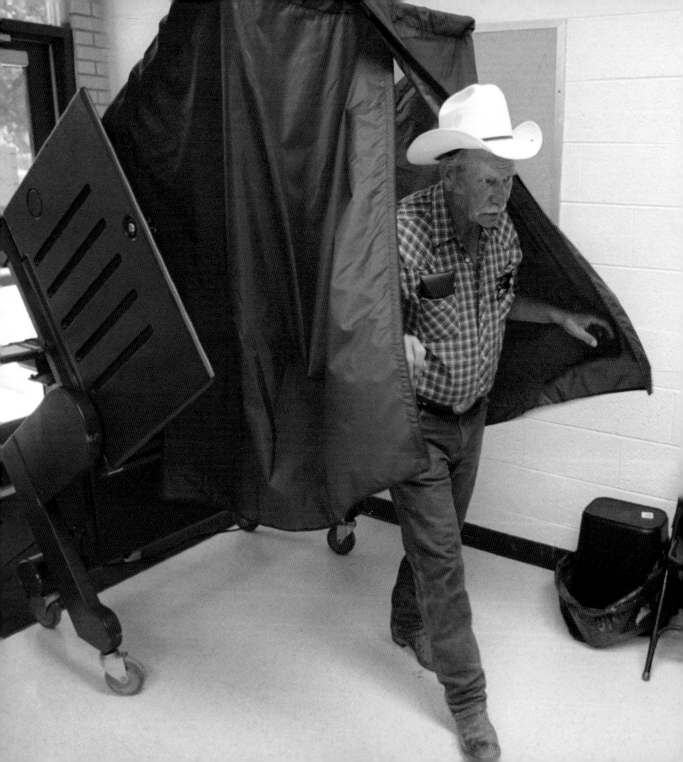

Power of the People

The people of the state also have a major voice in how government is run. First, all citizens aged eighteen and older can vote. They have the right to choose the candidate they think will do the most good for their state. In addition many state constitutions offer citizens the power to change laws and make new ones. They can do so in two ways, through **initiatives** and **referenda**.

A voter from New Mexico comes out of the voting booth after casting his ballot. Voting is one of the most important rights granted U.S. citizens.

An initiative is a bill written and presented to the legislature by a citizen or group of citizens. An initiative usually begins when a citizen draws up a petition, which is a written request. He or she then gets other citizens to sign the petition to show their support. If enough people sign the petition, the bill either goes before the legislature for a vote or it goes on a **ballot** for the state's voters to decide.

Petitions address issues people feel are important to their state. They can be the first step in creating or changing laws. Here, concerned citizens in California protest pollution in their state.

▶

A referendum is a law created by the state legislature and voted on by the people during a general election. If a majority of the state's voters is in favor of the referendum, it becomes a law. A referendum can also be used to amend, or change, the state constitution.

The legislature creates laws in many different ways, including by petition and referendum. These methods often require that citizens get involved, casting their vote for or against the new or changed laws.

If officials wish to change the state constitution, they must present a referendum to the people. Voters then have the chance to accept or reject the change. Some states also require citizens to vote on certain types of proposed laws. These include laws to increase taxes or change the boundaries, or borderlines, of a city.

Often the state legislature must get the approval of the voters before changing the state constitution. ▶

Making Your Mark

One way you can take part in state government is to contact your state senator or representative whenever an issue interests you. You can ask for information about the plans he or she has for the state and which bills he or she supports. You can give your opinion to your state officials about proposed laws or laws you think your state should adopt.

Every citizen can have a voice in his or her state government. Here, students tell U.S. senator Hillary Rodham Clinton about the health problems pollution can create.

You can find the names and addresses of your state legislators at your local library or on your state's Web page. Your voice counts! Express yourself, and maybe you can improve the lives of your friends, family, and the rest of the people who live in your state.

The senate chamber is where many of the state's important decisions are made. Maybe someday you will be sitting in one of these seats helping to pass a new state law. ▶

Glossary

ballot—The list of candidates or issues given to citizens who then cast their votes.

bicameral legislature—A state law-making body that has two houses, or parts.

census—A count of all the people who live in the United States.

constitution—The rules that tell the state government how it is supposed to do its work.

enact—To make into law.

executive branch—The branch of government that puts laws into action.

governor—The state's chief executive officer.

house of representatives—One part of the legislature. Most representatives serve terms of two years.

initiative—A proposal for a law that is created by citizens of a state to be voted on by the state legislature.

judicial branch—The branch of government that explains the law.

legislative branch—The branch of government that creates laws.

president pro tempore—The person who is second in command in the state senate.

procedure—A set of steps or a way of performing a task.

referendum—A proposal for a law created by citizens of a state and voted on during an election.

senate—One part of the legislature. Most senators serve terms of four years.

veto—To reject.

Find Out More

Books

Berry, Joy W. *Every Kid's Guide to Laws that Relate to Kids in the Community.* Broomall, PA: Children's Press, 1988.

———. *Every Kid's Guide to Laws that Relate to Parents and Children.* Broomall, PA: Children's Press, 1987.

Feinbert, Barbara Silberdick. *State Governments.* Danbury, CT: Franklin Watts, 1993.

Giesecke, Ernestine. *Local Government.* Portsmouth, NH: Heinemann, 2000.

———. *State Government.* Portsmouth, NH: Heinemann, 2000.

Santrey, Laurence. *State and Local Government.* New York: Troll, 1985.

Web Sites

Branches of Government Webquest
http://www.kn.pacbell.com/wired/fil/pages/webbranchessh.html

Government for Kids—State Government
http://www.govspot.com/state/

Great Government for Kids
http://www.cccoe.net/govern/

Learning about the Branches of Government
http://www.kidspoint.org/columns2.asp?column_id=358&column_type=homework

Also, many state government Web sites have a kids' page for the state's youngest citizens. Do a search for your state's official site or have your parents, teacher, or librarian help you.

Author's Bio

Suzanne LeVert is the author of many books for young readers on a host of different topics, including biographies of former Louisiana governor Huey Long and author Edgar Allan Poe. Most recently, she wrote four books in Benchmark Books' Kaleidoscope series on U.S. government, *The Congress, The Constitution, The President,* and *The Supreme Court.*

Index